Acknowledgments

Grateful acknowledgment is given to the authors, artists, photographers, museums, publishers, and agents for permission to reprint copyrighted material. Every effort has been made to secure the appropriate permission. If any omissions have been made or if corrections are required, please contact the Publisher.

LEXILE® is a trademark of MetaMetrics, Inc., and is registered in the United States and abroad. Copyright © 2018 MetaMetrics, Inc. All rights reserved.

This book has been officially leveled by using the F&P Text Level Gradient™ System. Neither Heinemann nor Fountas and Pinnell have produced, endorsed, or sponsored this product, nor are they affiliated with the Publisher or responsible for this product.

For product information and technology assistance, contact us at Customer & Sales Support, 888-915-3276

For permission to use material from this text or product, submit all requests online at
www.cengage.com/permissions

Further permissions questions can be emailed to
permissionrequest@cengage.com

National Geographic Learning | Cengage
1 Lower Ragsdale Drive
Building 1, Suite 200
Monterey, CA 93940

National Geographic Learning, a Cengage company, is a provider of quality core and supplemental educational materials for the PreK–12, adult education, and ELT markets. Cengage is a leading provider of customized learning solutions with employees residing in nearly 40 different countries and sales in more than 125 countries around the world. Find your local representative at **NGL.Cengage.com/RepFinder**.

Visit National Geographic Learning online at
NGL.Cengage.com/school

ISBN: 978-0-3570-4850-4

Printed in the United States of America

Print Number: 01
Print Year: 2018

What are you doing?

by Lada Kratky

illustrated by André Ceolin

NATIONAL GEOGRAPHIC LEARNING | CENGAGE

What are you doing?

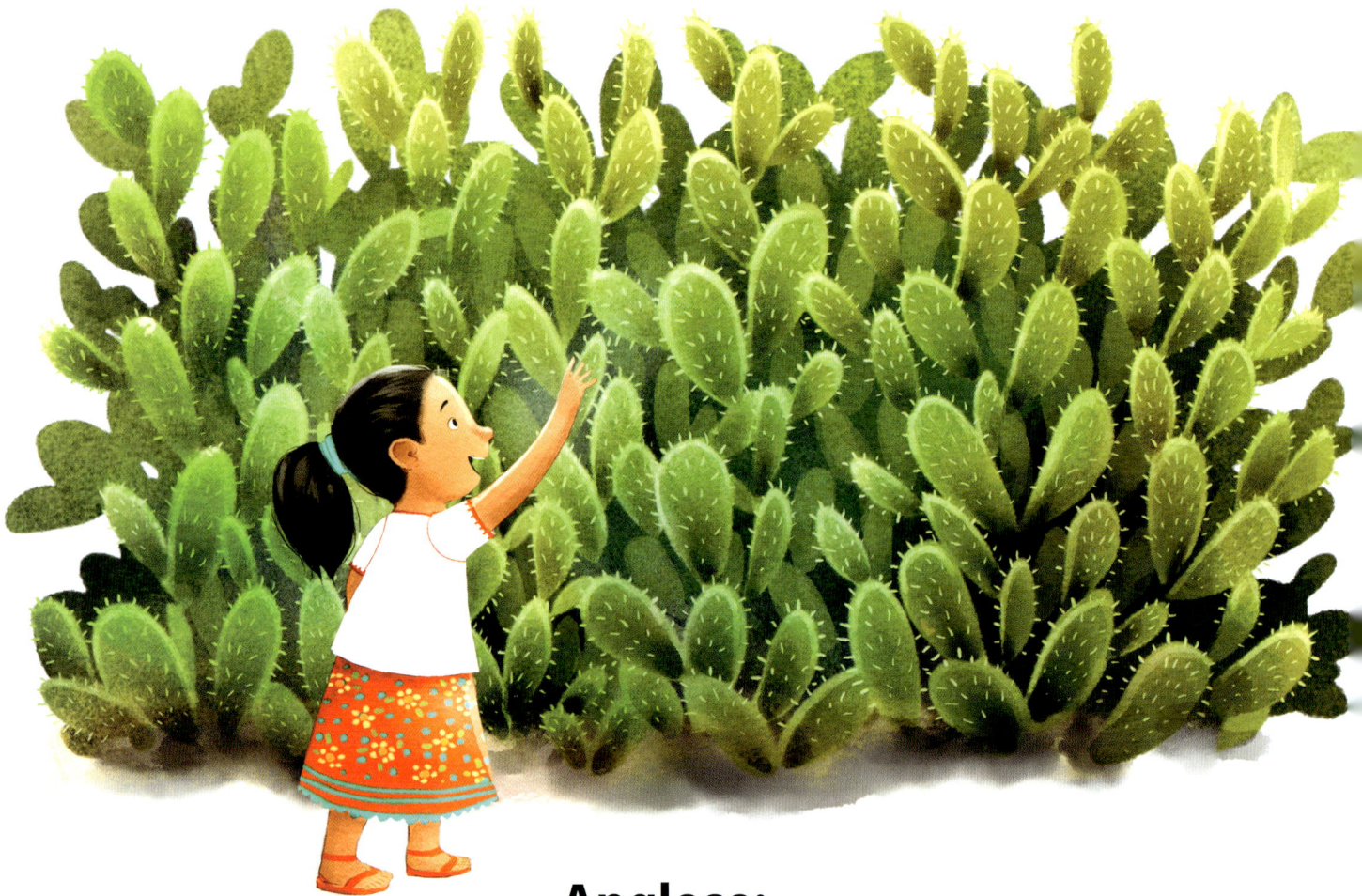

Analese:

What are you doing, Liador, Liador?

What are you doing, Liador?

Liador:

I'm planting corn, Analese, Analese.

In the furrows of my plot I'm planting corn.

Nicolás:

How do you plant it, Liador, Liador?

How do you plant it, Liador?

Liador:

I put a grain in a hole, Nicolás, Nicolás.

A little hole per step, nothing more, nothing less.

Alfonsín:

And now, what are you doing, Liador, Liador?

What are you doing now, Liador?

Liador:

I'm making tortillas, Alfonsín, Alfonsín.

Mountains of corn tortillas.

7

Helen:

How do you eat them, Liador, Liador?

How do you eat them, Liador?

Liador:

We eat them in empanadas, Helen, Helen.

They are so tasty they are fit for a queen.

9

Antón:

And now, what are you doing, Liador, Liador?

What are you doing now, Liador?

Liador:

Fresh lemon water, Antón, Antón.

I grate tender lemon in the molcajete.

Maribel:

And now, what are you doing, Liador, Liador?

What are you doing now, Liador?

Liador:

I'm cutting reeds, Maribel, Maribel,

For some baskets I'm going to weave.

Maribel:

What are the baskets for, Liador, Liador?

What are the baskets for, Liador?

Liador:

To keep clothes in, Maribel, Maribel.

To keep clothes in and also to sell.

Marisol:

And now, what are you doing, Liador, Liador?

What are you doing now, Liador?

Liador:

I'm embroidering shirts, Marisol, Marisol.

They look as pretty as a field of flowers.

Ruben:

And now, where are you going, Liador, Liador?

Where are you going now, Liador?

Liador:

I'm going to the market, Ruben, Ruben,

With tortillas, baskets and also shirts.

Don Ventura:

How much are the tortillas, Liador, Liador?

How much for the tortillas, Liador?

Liador:

They're a peso a dozen, don Ventura, don Ventura.

Tasty tortillas as round as the moon.

Iris:

How much are the baskets, Liador, Liador?

How much for the baskets, Liador?

Liador:

They're eight pesos each, Iris, Iris.

Colorful baskets like a brilliant rainbow.

Liador:

Now come, little children, to buy some shoes,

Notebooks and paper and pencils, too.

26

Liador:

Let's go home, little children, little children,

To eat empanadas with fresh lemon water.

Liador:

Who wants one, little children, little children?

Yuan:

I one! Yum!

Lupe:

I two! Yum!

Antonio:

I three!!! Yum…yum!